*Meditation, Ahhhahaha. The art of letting go, the complexity of simplicity. What-ever. Yes, there is beauty in seeking enlightenment and having an hour a day for reflection, but what about us... humans? Beginners, the ones who were not born into.. Buddhism. Meditation*

is a tool for developing a more peaceful life, growing into success and uncovering our genuine full potential. The side effects of meditation to lower stress and lower anxiety are uncanning. We are going to peer into the looking glass touching on how to open the doors to meditation.

Hold on for this condensed ride into your life for a healthier, more successful, more peaceful you!

I want inner peace, and serenity, success and throw some enlightenment on top please. There is a reason that Oprah, Katy Perry,

Hugh Jackman, Madonna, Paul McCartney, John Lennon and the list goes on and on, have all adopted meditation into their lifestyles. It is said that meditation aids in manifesting the life of your dreams, genuine to who you are. And, this is true. By acknowledging

who and what we are not
we begin to see what
exactly we are, and how
our qualities contribute to
the world we are part of.
We are going to look at
three things; How to prep
for meditation, Known ways
of meditation and how to
allow meditation to open
the doors to the life you

*truly dream of. With the cherry on top that if we are to develop these practices to pass onto our children to adopt for the next generation imagine the peaceful and fulfilling way of life we are setting the foundation for generations to come. "In moments of madness, meditation has helped me find moments of serenity -- and I would like to think that it would help provide young people a quite haven in a not-so-quite world" - Paul McCartney. For us developing into meditation not only allows us to live in peace, and opens the doors for opportunity but also for the next generation to come. And for this shift, I am most looking forward to.*

*## Chapter 1 Prep for Meditation*

*A mindset to get ready for meditation: There are numerous forms, methods, techniques and* practices for meditation. For myself and beginning family and friends this has helped and can be easily adopted and altered. Reminding ourselves that meditation is a time fore relaxation, a time to accept and to take a step back from being part of the commotion. Here we are *becoming an observer of all happenings in our lives that we experience. We are stepping out of our everyday happenings, we are detaching and looking at our lives from a distance. We are realizing that any expectations or assumptions we have are truly, pointless. We are* acknowledging we have no control over anything outside of ourselves. The only thing within our control is how we respond and choose to feel about any given circumstance. Here we are creating for ourselves a mental sanctuary. Here we see life that we experience as a passing *event, and see how we choose to perceive any situation can be peaceful. Here you are creating a mental space where not even you can bring your own worries, because here is your place to pier in on your own world from a distance. "Meditation is all about the pursuit of* nothingness. Its like the ultimate rest. Its better than the best sleep you've ever had. It's a quieting of the mind. It sharpens everything, especially your appreciation of your surrounding. It keeps life fresh." -Hugh Jackman. All of our learned responses, and learned *expectations create a mindset that does not allow us to respond in a way that is true to who we are or want to be and in many cases leads to a way of living what is stressful. The list of individuals who are recognized globally do not all practice meditation by* coincidence. Expanding to a mindset that who we are will truly blossom if only for us to drop our own ways, find mental space for peace and clarity and allow our world to respond back to us being a more peaceful, nonreactive individual.

*Prepping our minds to a state of accepting and responding rather than assuming and reacting takes practice, a practice very well worth the rewarding journey. Prepare that your mind may and most likely will drift and float coming and going into scenarios and or past or present or* even future circumstances. This is very common, simply remind yourself to come back to experiencing, come back to accepting what is and an open allowing mindset. Know that this is a health and lifelong journey of peace, this is a gift to yourself.

## Chapter 2 Meditations

As we mentioned there are numerous ways to meditate. Trial and error into a way that best works for yourself is encouraged. The best way to start is to just, start. Everywhere I have lived Wisconsin, California, Florida, Germany, Taiwan,

Thailand, Indonesia and places traveled in between, in all these locations I have found open groups of meditation, all varying in type. Along with YouTube as a good source for guided meditations on all sorts. Transcendental, Heart Rythme, Kundalini, guided, visualization,

Qigong, Zazen, mindfulness
these are a few of the
different forms of
meditation commonly
practiced. However, to sit
or lay with a guided
meditation on YouTube is
one of my go to's. It all
depends on where your
mind is at and what you are
drawn to experience. The
best way to

experience is to just, start. Pick one and/or look up local meditation classes or groups and try it out.

What ever you choose know that meditation is a practice, and like anything we are new to there is trial and error, learning and growth. A common root among the well known names we mentioned is a progression in meditation. "A man is but a product of his thoughts, what he thinks he becomes." - Mahatma Gandhi. Our minds create our reality, how we view the world, and how we perceive ourselves can

entrap us or be a peaceful
and freeing way of life.

As I told myself when I first
started meditating; try it
for one week. Maybe ten
minutes everyday, I did not
put a goal of how long but
just to start once everyday.
To take that first calming
breath and see where it

*leads. I told this to myself because the idea of letting go of my own assumptions, expectations and way of thinking sounded daunting. But to tell myself just for this week I will see if this adds a moment of a more peaceful mindset, and self growth or enjoyment. If it doesn't add a healthier aspect after that week I can*

always just, stop. And here
I am years later.


## Chapter 3 Letting
## Meditation Work

If you want to fly, give up
everything that weighs you
down. sounds easy...right?
Our minds can create
paradise, or struggle. Many
times we find so much

comfort in a way of operating or thinking that we are so used to that even to our own destruction or at our own expense, we still don't challenge these ways of operating. Many times we sit in our own discomfort because it is what we have become used to for years. Letting meditation work is a self challenge to let go of our way of thinking that we have known and become accustomed to for so long. Seeing that you have an anchor within your belief system that holds you back, limits, and keeps you in situations or brings you experiencing the same unwanted circumstances is the first freeing step. The *more we break down our own thinking patterns and how they produce a pattern within our lives, the closer we get to understanding by opening our minds to accept new ways of thinking and develop a new belief system we will attract a new way of living.*

*By allowing meditation to*

work we are simply stepping back, letting go of the steering wheel and choosing to not react but choosing to allow ourselves to experience life and respond in a manner that will lead to a more fulfilling and harmonious existence.

Here we have touched on just the beginning of your

meditation journey.
Remember it is just that,
your self journey to
developing and iving a
more peaceful, rewarding
and authentic life.

If you are looking for more resources for building your foundation checkout:

Instagram: _Just.b___

Facebook: @just.b.llc

YouTube: Britney Anne

YouTube: Just.b The Island

Thank you for the courage to explore and grow your authentic self.

I am very excited for you on your journey!
-Britney Anne Klump

Made in the USA
Columbia, SC
05 April 2023

14387027R00020